Glory of Steam

Jubilee 4-6-0 No. 45593 *Kolhapur* faces a Black 5 across the turntable at Holbeck

Glory of Steam

Eric Treacy

LONDON

IAN ALLAN LTD

First published 1969

Reprinted 1981

ISBN 0 7110 1171 0

Published by Ian Allan Ltd, Shepperton, Surrey; and printed by Ian Allan Printing Ltd at their works at Coombelands in Runnymede, England

Introduction

I AM GOING to play a dirty trick on the reviewers (if any) of this book. I am going to review it myself!

"In this, his last book of photographs of the steam engine, Eric Treacy has produced a book tediously like his previous efforts. Those who looked for something new or original will be disappointed, for here is a selection of pictures, many of which are well known to readers of railway periodicals. There is much repetition of some of the locomotives now in private ownership, there is a preponderance of the conventional three-quarter view. There are serious gaps in the types of locomotives depicted, and an undue emphasis on scenes in the north. At least, we can say, there is much for those who want to see the steam engine at work, and for this we are grateful, but we cannot resist the impression that Treacy has obviously scraped the barrel in this book. He says that it is to be his last, and we are bound to say that it ought to be!".

* * *

During the recent Lambeth Conference of Anglican Bishops, a certain Bishop from north of the Border stole away one afternoon to visit the Transport Museum at Clapham. When I met him next morning, he confided to me that he wished that he had never gone.

"Why?" said I.

"It was awful," he said, "to see those magnificent machines standing there cold and dead: they weren't built as exhibits, but to work. I wish I'd never gone."

I know what he meant. An exhibition of dead engines is a bit like a cemetery.

I have tried in this collection of pictures to show the steam locomotive at work. As I look at these pictures with the affectionate eye of the one who took them, so much comes back to me. I hear sounds, I smell smells, that will for ever be precious to me.

I have included many pictures which may be familiar to those who have known my work during the last 30 years. I have done so, because, (a) many people have written and asked me to, (b) because books in which they originally appeared are now out of print, and (c) because I thought that they really did depict the "Glory of Steam".

* * *

"So much comes back to me . . . ."

For instance—the scene at a country station (now closed and gone for ever) in Cumberland.

The sort of station where seemingly little ever happened, and the arrival of a train was something of an event. Stations where the Station Master didn't wear a top hat, but had time to talk, and was often to be found in his shirt sleeves tending the station garden, or feeding his hens. I remember spending a very happy afternoon at such a station about 30 years ago. The sun shone out of a blue sky: a small beck gurgled under a bridge at the end of the platform; in the Station Yard the local kids were chasing each other with a good deal of noise; in the near-by fields the cattle made those deep throated noises peculiar to cattle; the signalman sat on the steps of his box reading the newspaper; and in the booking office the kettle was boiling on the gas ring in preparation for the afternoon "cuppa".

Above, the birds sang: below, the bees buzzed and the crickets chirped.

Then into this idyllic scene there comes the imperious ring of the signal bell.

In a flash—everything changes!

The signalman drops his paper.

A lot more ringing takes place.

One by one, the signal arms drop.

A hush falls, there is an air of expectation.

The kids stop chasing each other; even the cattle start to eye the line with a bleary and grudging interest.

The congregation gathers.

Old gentlemen appear from the village, the postman, the village policeman, farm-labourers, a host of people, previously invisible, appear at a variety of vantage points along the line—sitting on gates, looking over bridges, leaning against fences.

All seems set for something big to happen.

In a flash, it does.

The "Coronation Scot", gleaming in the sunshine, framed momentarily in the arch of a bridge, hurls itself through the station.

We get an impression rather than a view—of smoke, gleaming paint—blue and silver; throbbing movement; and while we are trying to sort out our impressions, the train is gone.

Then followed a certain anti-climax. For the Village the big event had come and gone. Slowly, the scene reverted to its earlier peace—the more so because someone had taken the kettle off and made the tea. Like a motion picture that has been stopped and started again, all the characters in the scene start doing again what they were doing when this steaming Hercules burst upon them.

And I tilt my hat over my nose and am relaxing once again on the hard station seat when there comes the sort of friendly call that is so typical of the country and its kindness—

"What about a cup o' tea, Mister?"

Yes—those country stations had a charm all their own. Part of the charm was that they weren't as blasé as the big stations. The "Coronation Scot" could pass through Crewe without anyone appearing to notice it; but in the country they knew how to be excited. They were capable of appreciating things that ought to be appreciated. And—they didn't worry about platform tickets!

* * *

So much comes back to me ....

That tea room off the Great Hall at Euston, where they used to "mash" the best China tea anywhere in England.

And while we are talking about tea, there comes to me the memory of cold tea gulped from the driver's billy-can on the footplate of a re-built Scot at the top of the hill from Settle. A very hot day, very strong tea, and a very dry throat.

There comes back to me ....

The sulphurous smell of an engine shed; the fishy smell of a guard's van; the oily smell of the porters' room; the hot smell of a steam locomotive at the end of its journey.

There comes back to me ......

The friendly noise of a shunting engine during the long and wakeful hours of the night; the noise of coal being broken in the tender as the engine awaits its job. The wailing hooter of a Stanier Pacific as it storms through the Lune Valley and hurls itself through Tebay Station on the approaches to Shap: the sound of a signal bell tinkling in a nearby box, of the heavy thud of a signal lever being operated . . .

Sight, smells, and sounds—thus come our memories and impressions. The only one of the three that we cannot re-capture is the "smell" of the railway in the days of steam. Thanks to the camera and the tape recorder, the steam enthusiast can call back the great days of steam.

* * *

So, I come to the end of my prologue, which I fear may sound more like an epitaph.

This book is a tribute "in affection". I have heard many funeral orations which magnified the virtues of the departed, and tactfully overlooked his failings. I am sure that we enthusiasts are guilty of precisely this, and that we must provoke a good deal of irritation on the part of the professional railwaymen who have cursed the filth of the steam engine, who have sustained physical injuries in their contacts with it: men who have been near suffocated with ash, who have gasped on the footplate in the foul air of a long tunnel, who have endured the terror of a blow-back on the footplate: men who have been shaken to bits on some piece of run down machinery, who have had their top ends frozen, and their lower ends roasted, on the footplate. Men who have developed a love-hate relationship with this handsome, often stubborn, monster.

Yet, for all this, how many of the legends about the steam engine have originated with the men who handled them. A gathering of drivers who have worked on steam will have one subject of conversation—the steam engine. Curious, the spell it exercises over the men who, in their time, have been infuriated injured, and fascinated by it.

Huffing and puffing, dirty or clean, blowing off or quietly simmering, slipping or priming, shunter or "special", in shed or station, blasting up hill, or coasting down hill,—the toast is—The Steam Engine. Or perhaps, a vote of thanks is more appropriate than a toast: thanks for the pleasure that it has brought to my generation, not so much for what it did, as for what it was.

Brute it was, that poured out its heart in smoke and steam, and made music for those with ears to hear.

* * *

I would wish my last words to be in the nature of salute to the new generation of engine-men.

We who sentimentalise about the steam engine, and those who handled it, must sometimes seem to imply that all greatness is passed, that all character is gone. This is, clearly, nonsense.

Admittedly, much that is colourful has gone. No longer is there the link between a particular shed, its engines and the men that work them. No longer do we spot old Alf Cartwright, Gilbert Crossley, Bill Hoole, Ted Hailstone, an' all—with their heads stuck out of the cab on the morning train to London. No longer do we see the driver and his mate mooching round the streets of our cities in between turns, their rations in an old respirator case, their overalls and headgear being an unmistakable uniform—all this has gone, and we are the poorer for it.

The modern driver is clean, and to my ageing eyes, astonishingly youthful; at the end of the journey he melts into the crowd of hurrying passengers: but, make no mistake, he is playing his full part in the creation of a superb railway system.

The old brigade of drivers had it tough, and they enjoyed it. The new style driver may not have the same tough conditions of exposure and rough-riding with which to contend, but he has a job demanding great steadiness of nerve, and instant reaction. Driving trains of 300–400 tons at sustained speeds of 100 m.p.h. calls for qualities of technical skill as great as any that were demanded of their predecessors.

Let us not forget, too, the large number of footplate staff, who, comparatively late in life, have had to convert from steam to electric and diesel-electric motive power. It has not been easy for men in late middle age to learn completely new techniques, but most of them have done superbly well, and are, from all accounts, enjoying it.

No, we must not so give ourselves up to sentimentality and nostalgia that we fail to see how successful footplate staff have been in accepting the great change-over. We rejoice in the much more comfortable conditions that they now enjoy, and, at the same time, recognise them as the true descendents of those splendid railwaymen who raced from London to Aberdeen, who did their wonderful "bit" with steam in the two great Wars, and whose weather-beaten and cheerful faces we no longer see stuck out of the cab side as they bring their trains safely to their journey's end.

Eric Treacy

TO

Mary Leyland Treacy

IN LOVE AND GRATITUDE

who for 36 years has endured the vicissitudes of being married to a railway enthusiast. This book is a tribute for years of unselfish endurance and patience.

Quartette of Liverpool lads pay homage to the steam locomotive at Edge Hill Sheds. Stanier Pacific No. 6254 *City of Stoke-on-Trent.*

Stanier Pacific No. 46227 *Duchess of Devonshire* waits at Carlisle with a stopping train for Glasgow

Left: View from the tender of Stanier Pacific No. 46240 *City of Coventry* approaching Shap Summit with the down "Royal Scot"

Right: One of Stanier's class 5 mixed traffic engines nears Shap Summit with a freight train

Left: Unrebuilt Royal Scot 4-6-0 No. 6104 *Scottish Borderer* leans to the curve at Thrimby Grange with a train from Glasgow to Birmingham

Right: British Railways Britannia Pacific No. 70050 *Firth of Clyde* passes Harrison's Lime Works with a Glasgow to Manchester train

ROYAL SCOT

Above: Pacific No. 46240 *City of Coventry* winds through the woods at Strickland with the up "Royal Scot"

Left: The Birmingham "Scot" at Harthope on the climb to Beattock Summit. Pacific No. 46203 *Princess Margaret Rose*

BACHELORS BUTTON
60537
70035
46237

Left top: A2 Peppercorn Pacific No. 60537 *Bachelor's Button* on the turntable at Haymarket, Edinburgh

Left centre: Britannia Pacific No. 70035 *Rudyard Kipling* at York

Left bottom: Stanier Pacific No. 46237 *City of Bristol* at Carlisle, Upperby with an up "Royal Scot"

Above: A1 Pacific 60129 *Guy Mannering* at Newcastle Central

Above: A well known, but popular picture. Rebuilt Scot No. 6117 *Welsh Guardsman* leaves Carlisle with the down "Thames-Clyde Express"

Below: The down "Waverley" express passes Gargrave, north of Skipton. Jubilee 4-6-0 No. 45691 *Orion* pilots Jubilee No. 45573 *Newfoundland*

THE WAVERLEY
45691
60

Jubilee No. 5671 *Prince Rupert* passes Whitmore Station with the "Pines Express"

Above: Last day of steam from Bradford, Forster Square. Jubilee No. 45593 *Kolhapur* with fitted freight train for Heysham

Below: At Tyseley Motive Power Depot. Mr. P. B. Whitehouse's two engines, No. 7029 *Clun Castle*, and No. 5593 *Kolhapur*

Summer's morning at Leeds. 1. Gresley Pacific No. 60003 *Andrew K. McCosh* approaches the camera

Summer's morning at Leeds. 2. The same engine passes the camera and heads for Wakefield

Right: Privately owned A4 Pacific No. 4498 *Sir Nigel Gresley* at York Motive Power Depot

Below: The same engine receives attention on the turntable at York

Above: *Sir Nigel Gresley* leaves Carlisle, Kingmoor with an excursion for Newcastle

Left: A4 Pacific No. 4498 changes direction at Carlisle, Upperby

In the shed at Carlisle, Kingmoor

Two gleaming Jubilees at Holbeck Motive Power Depot

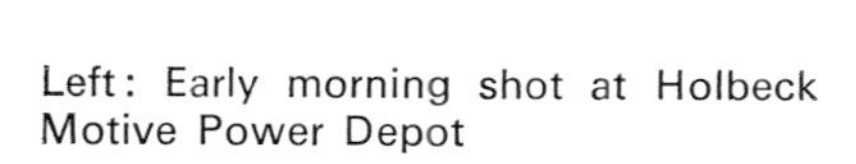
Left: Early morning shot at Holbeck Motive Power Depot

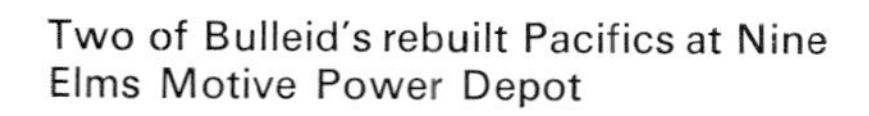
Two of Bulleid's rebuilt Pacifics at Nine Elms Motive Power Depot

Above: The glory that was the LNER. 1 Gresley's A3 Pacific No. 4472 *Flying Scotsman*, now owned by Mr. Alan Pegler, at Crewe South Shed

Below: The glory that was the LNER. 2 Gresley's A4 Pacific No. 4498 *Sir Nigel Gresley*, now in the ownership of the A4 Society at Crewe South Shed

SIR NIGEL GRESLEY
Nº 4498
A 4
KINGS +

45593

N°
CLASS
K4

Left top: Stanier Jubilee 4-6-0 No. 45593 *Kolhapur* at Holbeck

Left bottom: Lord Garnock's engine K4 2-6-0 No. 3442 *The Great Marquess* at Leeds City Station

Above: Stanier's class 5MT engine No. 45428 at Holbeck

Left: A4 Pacific No. 60009 *Union of South Africa* at Kings Cross with the down "Capitals Limited"

Right: Excursion arranged by the Railway Magazine in celebration of their 50 years existence threads York Station behind A3 No. 4472 *Flying Scotsman*

Below: A3 Pacific No. 60077 *The White Knight* leaves York with a train for Newcastle

THE HADRIAN FLYER
No 4472

ROYAL SCOT
46230
THE
ROYAL SCOT
46236

7002
5704

Left top: Stanier Pacific No. 46230 *Duchess of Buccleuch* comes off the up "Royal Scot" at Carlisle, and No. 46236 *City of Bradford* waits to take the train on to London

Above: A3 Pacific No. 4472 *Flying Scotsman* (not in steam) is taken for a drink at Doncaster by a B1 4-6-0

Left bottom: At Edge Hill, Liverpool. 0-4-0 saddle tank engine No. 7002 built by Kitson's, stands beside Jubilee 4-6-0 No. 5704 *Leviathan*

60073
20

Left top: A3 Pacific No. 60073 *St. Gatien* with a train from Liverpool to Newcastle at Wortley Junction, Leeds, passes a 2-6-4 tank engine bringing a train from Ilkley into Leeds

Left bottom: One of Stanier's streamlined Pacifics No. 6223 *Princess Alice* at Edge Hill en route for Lime Street

Above: Trio at Carlisle Citadel, left to right; Stanier Pacific No. 46244 *King George VI,* Jubilee 4-6-0 No. 45724 *Warspite* and Princess Pacific No. 46201 *Princess Elizabeth*

46203

Princess Pacific No. 46212 *Duchess of Kent* at Wavertree with the 5.25 p.m. from Liverpool Lime Street to Euston

Far left: Pacific No. 46203 *Princess Margaret Rose* at Clifton with a train from Glasgow to Birmingham

The one and only! The Turbomotive No. 6202 at Wavertree with an up express from Liverpool

Above: A Castle in the North Eastern Region. No. 7029 *Clun Castle* at Wortley Junction, near Leeds, with an enthusiasts' excursion to Carlisle

Below: Another enthusiasts' special. A4 Pacific No. 4498 *Sir Nigel Gresley* slowing down in York Station to change crews on its way to Newcastle. (Did they have enough coal?)

N° 4498

Up "Royal Scot" in the Clyde Valley at Crawford. Stanier Pacific No. 46223 *Princess Alice*

Right: Rebuilt Scot passing Greskine Box on Beattock with a stopping train from Carlisle to Glasgow. No. 46104 *Scottish Borderer*

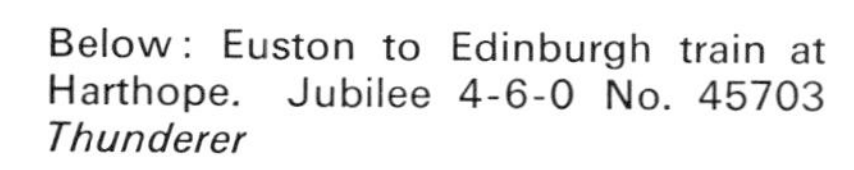

Below: Euston to Edinburgh train at Harthope. Jubilee 4-6-0 No. 45703 *Thunderer*

"White Rose" 1. The down "White Rose" leaves King's Cross. A1 Pacific No. 60136 *Alcazar*

"White Rose" 2. Up "White Rose" at Wortley South. A3 Pacific No. 60107 *Royal Lancer* with appropriate embellishment

"White Rose" 3. Up "White Rose" at the same place. A3 Pacific No. 60055 *Woolwinder,* before improvements

Above: Afternoon procession from Holbeck to Leeds City. Jubilee No. 45590 *Travancore* and Britannia Pacific No. 70016 *Ariel* to work the up and down "Thames-Clydes", and a class 2 4-4-0

Below: In the murk of Liverpool Street Station, Britannia No. 70001 *Lord Hurcomb* waits with the down "Norfolkman"

8145

Above: Class 8F 2-8-0 No. 8145 at Gargrave with a down freight

Below: In the valley of the Aire, class 4F 0-6-0 No. 4222 between Steeton and Keighley with a freight for Stourton

92026
15
A

Above: A3 Pacific No. 60037 *Hyperion* in Newcastle Central with the down "Flying Scotsman"

Left: Class 9F 2-10-0 No. 92026 fitted with Franco-Crosti boiler in Holbeck Shed

Above: A3 Pacific No. 60077 *The White Knight* leaves York with a train for Newcastle

Left: WD 2-8-0 No. 90116 draws away from Wakefield, Kirkgate with a freight for Healey Mills

Below: A2 No. 60531 *Barham* leaves York with a train for Edinburgh as V2 2-6-2 No. 60979 heads a train of empty stock

Above: Bunch of Patriots 1. No. 45513 nears Shap Summit with a train from Blackpool to Glasgow

Left: Bunch of Patriots 2. No. 45535 *Sir Herbert Walker* in the Holbeck Shed

Bunch of Patriots 3. No. 45501 *St. Dunstans* pilots a rebuilt Scot out of Leeds City with a train from Newcastle to Liverpool

Above: Freight on Beattock 1. Jubilee No. 45724 *Warspite* at Greskine

Right top: Freight on Beattock 2. Stanier Class 5MT leaves Beattock Station after taking on a banker

Right bottom: Freight on Beattock 3. Class 5MT 2-6-0 No. 42780 at Harthope

44953

42780

Above: Moguls 1. K2/2 2-6-0 No. 61788 *Loch Rannoch* leaves Fort William with a train for Mallaig

Right: Moguls 3. Gresley K4 No. 61996 *Lord of the Isles* near Spean Bridge with a freight train

Below: Moguls 2. Class 5MT 2-6-0 No. 42766 at Gledholt, Huddersfield with empty stock

61996

Above: The down "Royal Scot" climbs Beattock. Rebuilt Scot No. 46121 *Highland Light Infantry*

Below: The up "Irish Mail" leaves Holyhead. Rebuilt Scot No. 46166 *London Rifle Brigade*

46166
L M S
46166

Smoke over Carlisle! Stanier Pacific No. 46221 *Queen Elizabeth* at Carlisle Citadel with the down "Royal Scot"

Stanier Pacific No. 46244 *King George VI* crosses the Harthope Viaduct, Beattock, with a train for Perth

Princess Pacific No. 46210 *Lady Patricia* starts the climb to Beattock Summit with the Euston–Glasgow sleeper

L M S
5593

Above: Visit to Tyseley 1. Castle 4-6-0 No. 7029 *Clun Castle*

Left top: Visit to Tyseley 2. Jubilee 4-6-0 No. 5593 *Kolhapur* in LMS red on the turntable

Left bottom: Visit to Tyseley 3. *Clun Castle* follows *Kolhapur* into the shed

Above: *Clun Castle* visits York 1. August 1967

Left: *Clun Castle* visits York 2. October 1967. Mr. Patrick Whitehouse, the owner, in right foreground

Right: *Clun Castle* visits York 3. Nose to nose *Clun Castle* greets A4 No. 60019 *Bittern*

Below: *Clun Castle* visits York 4. The "Castle" rumbles onto the turntable in York Shed

60037

Above: Bulleid West Country Pacific No. 21C140 leaves Victoria with the down "Golden Arrow"

Left: Passing Haymarket Sheds, Edinburgh, A3 No 60037 *Hyperion* with Edinburgh to Glasgow train

Above: A1 Pacific No. 60162 *Saint Johnstoun* threads through Princes Street Gardens, Edinburgh, with a train for Aberdeen

Right top: Departure from King's Cross. A1 Pacific No. 60158 (later named *Aberdonian*) heads north with a Newcastle train

Right bottom: Class N2 0-6-2T No. 69495 leaves King's Cross with a train for Hertford

60158

69495
HERTFORD
69495

Above: Royal Scot engine before rebuilding. No. 6130 *West Yorkshire Regiment* at Wavertree with an afternoon train for Euston

Below: Royal Scot engine after rebuilding. No. 6103 *Royal Scots Fusilier* between Bingley and Keighley with the down "Thames-Clyde"

6103
6103
L M S

Sight no more to be seen. Driver Arthur Rose of Holbeck looks out of the cab of Jubilee No. 45657 *Tyrwhitt*

Above: Class 8F 2-8-0 No. 48708 at Carlisle, Kingmoor

Below: Class WD 2-8-0 No. 90070 fills up at York

Left: Shap 1. Rebuilt Claughton 4-6-0 *Breadalbane*

Right: Shap 3. Locomotive exchanges. Bulleid Pacific No. 35017 *Belgian Marine* with down "Royal Scot"

Left: Shap 2. Royal Scot 4-6-0 No. 6116 *Irish Guardsman* with the Birmingham–Edinburgh–Glasgow express

Right: Shap 4. Stanier Pacific No. 46228 *Duchess of Rutland* at Scout Green with down "Midday Scot"

SOUTHERN
35017
46228

44878

Three shots in Holbeck Motive Power Depot

Class 5MT 4-6-0 passing Kingmoor Motive Power Depot with a mixed freight for Dumfries

Class 4P 3-cylinder Compound 4-4-0 No. 40919 leaves Carlisle Citadel with a train for Dumfries

Birmingham to Glasgow train at Etterby. Stanier Pacific No. 46257 *City of Salford*

Up Waverley express heads south from Carlisle. Black 5 pilots Jubilee 4-6-0 No. 45564 *New South Wales*

Class 4MT 2-6-4T No. 80061 leaves Stirling with empty stock

BR Pacifics 1. No. 70052 *Firth of Tay* leaves Carlisle Citadel with a train for Manchester

BR Pacifics 2. No. 72001 *Clan Cameron* climbs Beattock with a stopping train for Glasgow

A3 Pacific No. 60081 *Shotover* gets away from Keighley with a Leeds to Glasgow train

Southern Lord Nelson class 4-6-0 No. 863 *Lord Rodney*

Stanier Pacific No. 46255 *City of Hereford*

Morning at Beeston. V2 2-6-2 No. 60936 passes Beeston signal box with a train from Leeds to Doncaster and East Anglia

Evening at Holbeck. V2 2-6-2 No. 60886 at Holbeck Low Level with a train from Liverpool to Newcastle

Above: A4 No. 60031 *Golden Plover* noses into Copenhagen Tunnel before backing down for duty at King's Cross

Left: The down "Coronation" emerges from Potters Bar Tunnel. A4 Pacific No. 2510 *Silver Link*

Morning train to Leeds and Bradford. A4 Pacific No. 60017 *Silver Fox*

Up "Elizabethan" departs from Edinburgh Waverley. A4 Pacific No. 60012 *Commonwealth of Australia*

46233

W282

Above: Princess Pacific No. 46211 *Queen Maud* near Beattock Summit with an express to Glasgow

Left top: Stanier Pacific labours up Shap from the north with the up mid-day Scot. No. 46233 *Duchess of Sutherland*

Left bottom: Britannia Pacific in the Lune Valley. No. 70051, *Firth of Forth* with a Glasgow to Manchester train

Right: Clan Pacific No. 72002 *Clan Campbell* near Low Gill with an excursion from Glasgow to Blackpool

Above: Down "Golden Arrow" Pullman leaves Victoria. Lord Nelson class 4-6-0 No. 862 *Lord Collingwood*

Left: *Clun Castle* creeps into York Shed after a visit to Newcastle

Below: Jubilee 4-6-0 No. 45688 *Polyphemus* at Euston

Right: The down "Flying Scotsman" between the tunnels at King's Cross. A4 Pacific No. 60015 *Quicksilver*

Below: Train from west of England to Liverpool and Manchester leaves Shrewsbury. Pacific No. 46255 *City of Hereford*

46255
46255

Left: *Clun Castle* in the North 1. Front ends of *Clun Castle* and A4 No. 60019 *Bittern* in York Shed

Below: *Clun Castle* in the North 2. At Beeston, heads an Ian Allan Excursion to King's Cross

Clun Castle at Holbeck 1. Touching up before setting out for London

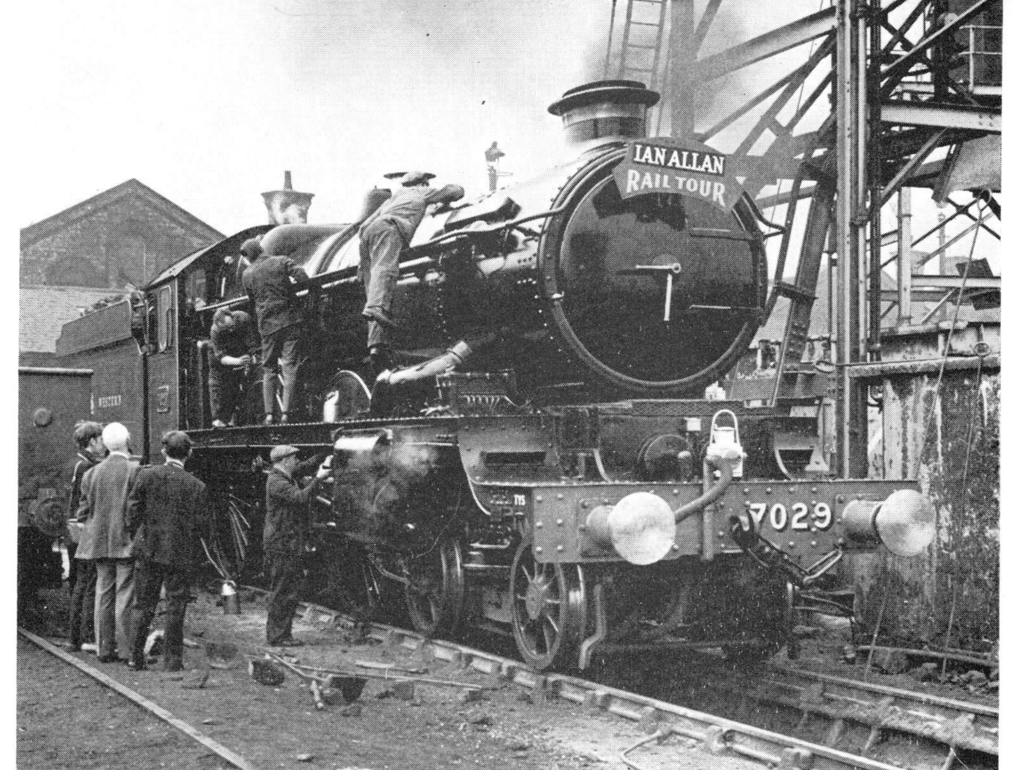

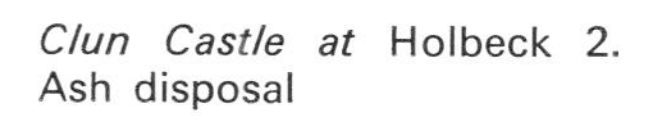
Clun Castle at Holbeck 2. Ash disposal

Left: B1 4-6-0 No. 61386 slogging up the hill from Leeds Central with a train for Doncaster

Right top: Jubilee *Kolhapur* at Forster Square, Bradford with mixed freight for Heysham

Right bottom: A4 Pacific No. 60010 *Dominion of Canada* at Tingley with morning train from Leeds to King's Cross

Below: Class 3MT 2-6-2T No. 82026 with Harrogate portion of train from London (Headlamps wrong!)

45593

60010

Above: Down "Flying Scotsman" gets away from Newcastle. A4 Pacific No. 60012 *Commonwealth of Australia*

Left: A train for Perth leaves Carlisle Citadel. Stanier Pacific No. 46226 *Duchess of Norfolk*

Locomotive exchanges. Bulleid Merchant Navy Pacific at Beeston with a train from Leeds to King's Cross. No. 35017 *Belgian Marine*

Above: North east wind beats across the valley. Rebuilt Scot No. 46145 *Duke of Wellington's Regiment* at Ais Gill with the up "Thames Clyde Express"

Right top: Class 5MT 4-6-0 No. 44749 fitted with Caprotti valve gear near Nantwich with a train from Liverpool and Manchester to the west of England

Right bottom: York to Bristol train leaves York. Jubilee 4-6-0 No. 45662 *Kempenfelt*

44749

45662

Black 5s 1. No. 44667 at Wortley Junction with a train from Leeds to Carnforth

Black 5s 2. No. 45085 at Greskine with northbound freight

St. Pancras to Edinburgh train at Marley Junction, Keighley. Jubilee 4-6-0 No. 5573 *Newfoundland*

Freight train on the Waverley route. A3 Pacific No. 60099 *Call Boy* at Kingmoor

Up "Merseyside" at Edge Hill. Royal Scot engine No. 6127 *Old Contemptibles*

Privately owned A4 Pacific No. 4498 *Sir Nigel Gresley* moves out of Kingmoor with an excursion for Newcastle

Below left: Castle No. 7029 *Clun Castle* receives attention in York Shed

Above: Bulleid West Country Pacific No. 34101 *Hartland* leaves Victoria with a boat express

Below right: The "Capitals Limited" pulls out of King's Cross. A4 Pacific No. 60009 *Union of South Africa*

CLUN CASTLE
THE CAPITALS LIMITED
60009
A·4
HAYMARKET

The "White Rose" 1. A3 Pacific No. 60046 *Diamond Jubilee* at Wakefield Westgate station

The "White Rose" 2. A4 Pacific No. 60007 *Sir Nigel Gresley* pulls up the bank from Leeds Central Station

The original "Trans-Pennine". Jubilee 4-6-0 No. 45695 *Minotaur* at Linthwaite with a train from Hull to Liverpool

Western Region 4300 class 2-6-0 No. 6340 near Chester with a freight train

Pickersgill 0-4-4T No. 55232 comes off the Moffat Branch at Beattock

Farewell Steam! A3 Pacific No. 60064 *Tagalie* takes leave of us at Rossington